Introductory Note

This Education for Socialists publication contains the transcript of a May 6, 1975, discussion led by Farrell Dobbs on problems of strategy and tactics in the struggle against fascism. The discussion has been edited by the participants for inclusion in this publication.

Farrell Dobbs is the author of *Teamster Rebellion*, *Teamster Power*, and *Teamster Politics*.* These works, published by Pathfinder Press, record Dobbs' experiences as a leader in the Minneapolis truck drivers' strikes of 1934, as the organizer of the campaign to unionize truck drivers throughout the Middle West, and as a participant in socialist efforts to build a class-struggle leadership of the Teamsters Union. Dobbs is a former national secretary of the Socialist Workers Party, and was the party's candidate for president in 1948, 1952, 1956, and 1960.

Other participants in the discussion included: Steve Clark, at that time the National Secretary of the Young Socialist Alliance (YSA); Ginny Hildebrand, at that time the National Organization Secretary of the YSA; George Novack, the outstanding Marxist author of *Pragmatism versus Marxism* and *Democracy and Revolution;* Doug Jenness and Betsey Stone, members of the National Committee of the Socialist Workers Party; and Jack Barnes, National Secretary of the Socialist Workers Party. After the December 1975 YSA Convention, Clark and Hildebrand left the YSA national leadership to join the staff of the revolutionary-socialist newsweekly, the *Militant*.

The discussion was sparked by an incident at San Francisco State University in March 1975. A professor invited a member of the National Socialist White People's Party, a fascist group that apes Hitler's storm troopers, to speak before a speech class. Ultra left groups organized a small confrontationist demonstration that successfully forced cancellation of the talk. Most of the campus community reacted with hostility to the demonstration, which students saw as a violation of freedom of speech. Taking advantage of this atmosphere, the university administration launched an effort (ultimately unsuccessful) to expel several radical and socialist groups from the campus.

The campus chapter of the Young Socialist Alliance issued a leaflet that opposed the victimizations while criticizing the ill-chosen tactics of the ultralefts. In line with a policy adopted by the YSA at the July 1974 Plenum of its National Committee, the leaflet held that fascists had no right to speak at the university.

The incident in San Francisco sparked a reconsideration by the YSA leadership of the advisability of opposing democratic rights for fascists. They discovered that the Socialist Workers Party, together with Leon Trotsky, had long held that slogans that denied anyone's right to free speech damaged the defense of democratic rights against fascist attacks and ultimately increased the likelihood of the repression of the oppressed and exploited.

In the course of re-evaluating the previous stance of the YSA on this point, some of the YSA leaders proposed a discussion with Farrell Dobbs and other party leaders on this. The result was the discussion reprinted in these pages.

On June 7–10, 1975, the YSA National Committee held a plenum. A report on the struggle against fascist and racist attacks was presented by YSA National Chairperson Malik Miah. After several hours of discussion, the report was approved. It reaffirmed the basic strategy of the YSA on the

---

* The concluding volume in the series, *Teamster Bureaucracy*, was published in 1977.

building of a mass movement in defense of democratic rights, while incorporating the view that these struggles should not call for the suppression of anyone's free speech. The report, entitled "Free Speech and the Fight Against the Ultraright," is reprinted in the Education for Socialists publication, *The Fight Against Fascism in the USA*. That volume can be viewed as a companion to this one.

One of those who played a major role in clarifying the thinking of the young revolutionists on how to fight fascism was Bob Chester. He was a political leader and educator of the Trotskyist movement for more than forty years. A member of the San Francisco branch of the Socialist Workers Party, he died at the age of 62 on June 22, 1975.

MAY 1976.

COUNTER-MOBILIZATION:
A Strategy to Fight Racist and Fascist Attacks
By Farrell Dobbs

FARRELL DOBBS: I think we should start by abstracting for the moment from the immediate situation and take a look at the fight against fascism in a broader, more fundamental sense. In the process of discussing that, we will come around to the immediate problem. It would be better to spend a little time looking into broader, more general, more basic aspects of the fight against fascism. I'm talking about the strategic concepts of this fight and some broad lines of tactics that flow from these concepts.

Fundamentally, what are you up against? Good generals are always very careful to try to perceive as accurately as they can what the situation is on the opposing side and what the enemy's line of approach is. It's always very important for the leaders of a combat force—that's what we're talking about now, a combat force—to know how to get ready for combat and also how not to go into combat foolishly and precipitously.

What is the tactic of the ruling class? How does the ruling class proceed when it's getting ready to utilize fascism? What they want at that point is to turn from the existing form of bourgeois rule to a ruthless fascist dictatorship. The objective is to crush the organizations and the combat capacity of the working class, the main opponent of the capitalist class.

In a given country at a particular time when the bourgeoisie opens this chapter, there will be one or another degree of democratic rights. Our situation is one where there are on the lawbooks a somewhat extensive body of formal democratic rights won by the masses in the history of the class struggle in the U.S. The approach of the ruling class is to begin to move toward a deterioration of those rights.

Their tactic is to protect the rights of the fascists while at the same time using fascist forces to try to keep others from exercising those rights. One of the forces used to implement this is that most malevolent of all the repressive instruments of capitalist rule, the police forces. The police structure is of a character that makes it a breeding ground for fascists.

You don't only have an army of capitalist cops that represses opponents of capitalism, you have a ripe recruiting ground for fascism itself. You not only have cops implementing ruling class orders in aiding the fascists, you have a police force that is honeycombed with fascists. In this country at this time it is not yet honeycombed, but there are plenty of reactionaries and racists there. The more the lines of confrontation deepen and sharpen, the more the tendency is for fascist formations to attract adherents within the police department. It's an important thing to keep in mind. Apart from the fact that the cops aren't neutral in the class struggle, but are neutral on the side of the capitalists, you will be facing a formation that has a lot of fascist-minded elements in it.

The line of the police is to defend the exercise of the formal democratic rights of the fascists, on the one hand, and not to "see" the violations of the democratic rights of the fascists' victims. Meanwhile, the cops take full advantage of any violation of bourgeois-democratic law that the antifascists may commit. In any kind of confrontation between antifascist and fascist forces, the basic line of the cops is to protect the fascists in any way they can and to join in the victimization of the antifascists.

Anybody that's purporting to develop a strategy and shape tactics to fight fascism and doesn't start with an understanding of what method your enemy is going to use, can fall into all kinds of traps. Such missteps disadvantage the antifascists and aid the fascist forces. They also make things easier for the repressive arms of the ruling structure that are abetting the fascists.

Let's be a little more specific about some of the problems that arise if we fail to understand the nature of the confrontation. Let's take the demand raised by some that the government ban the fascists from speaking. This implies that the masses can rely on the government to protect them from the fascists. But that's only the beginning of the negative aspect of this demand. Anybody with an ounce of perception can see immediately that when you rely upon the government to protect the victims of the fascists, you are sowing illusions about the readiness of the government to defend the exercise of the democratic rights that are incorporated in the bourgeois constitution. But the capitalist regime absolutely can't be relied on to do that job.

The minute you say that the government should stop the meeting, you have to say the next thing. Unless you're fatuous enough to believe that the government is going to act, you're still left with the question, what are you going to do when the government doesn't act.

The implicit logic is this: No matter what the situation is, no matter what the stage of development, this approach means that your objective is to prevent the fascists from speaking. Now what kind of problems does that posture lead to?

Let's assume for the moment that it is possible to develop a sufficient action in the concrete situation to limit or suppress the fascists' speech.

Now it's conceivably possible that enough pressure could be developed to make the ruling powers do a little something to curb the democratic rights of the fascists. Then you simply arrive at a new stage of the problem.

The capitalists are always looking for ways to contravene the formal democratic rights of the antifascists. Anything the government might do to interfere with the exercise of democratic rights by the fascists, they will at the same time apply to the left, to the antifascists.

In the section of *Teamster Politics* on the WPA strikes, I discussed the loyalty oath that Roosevelt imposed on the WPA workers as part of whittling down the rolls. As always happens in such cases, the oath proscribed from participation the German-American Bund and all communist organizations. They always strike against the left at the same time as they hit the right.

Then they tend to give less and less enforcement to the proscription against the right. The more intense the struggle becomes, the more they will be inclined to use their seeming neutrality in the class struggle as a cover for paying less and less attention to what the fascists are doing. The government will let them do what they damn please, while more and more using its authority to curb the rights of the left. Thus, even if the government does something in passing to curb the rights of the fascists, all that happens in the last analysis is that the rulers get a new pretext for attacking the anticapitalist forces. They will piously claim to be moving in a perfectly fairminded way against the "extremists" on both sides of the controversy.

Thus, by demanding that the government suppress the formal rights of the fascists, you create a whole new set of tactical problems for yourself. The government does nothing that would really cripple the attack of the fascists, so you still have the essential problem of fighting the fascists. However, you now have the additional problem of fighting to defend some of your own rights against new restrictions adopted by the bourgeois-democratic state supposedly against the fascists. As Napoleon said to one of his generals, one more victory like that and we'll be back in Paris.

This tactic of demanding that the fascists be prevented from speaking puts you at a disadvantage in other ways. Two categories of the population at large can become a problem here.

There are people in capitalist society who are professional civil libertarians. They not only believe in the Bill of Rights, but believe in it as a kind of mystical object of worship that stands above the realities of the class struggle. It looms in their eyes like a first cause uncaused, as remote from and unsullied by all the confusions and conflicts of class society as God is from the realities of life on this planet.

If you demand that the government suppress the freedom of speech of the fascists or declare your intention of suppressing it, you automatically put the civil libertarians on the other side. That will be so even though your real aims in the fight are to defend your democratic rights against the fascists. You make a new tactical problem for yourself.

To take another example, is it not true that if you fight on a campus around the demand that fascists should not be allowed to speak, you can get in the way of elevating the consciousness of the very students you are trying to reach? Part of the process of radicalization is that they don't want anybody to tell them who to listen to or what to think.

If you are insisting that fascists can't speak, you risk antagonizing students. You risk making them, not in the last analysis but in a formal sense at the given moment, into allies of the fascists. They are radicalizing and often are recruitable to the revolutionary movement, but instead they get jockeyed into a position that confuses them greatly. You wind up making another tactical problem for yourself.

The implication of confidence in the ability of the government to oppose the fascists and protect democratic rights is only the most obvious error in the demand to prevent fascists from speaking. You create problems that get in the way of mobilizing an ever broader mass opposition.

What, then, should be our line of approach? Let me refer here to our approach to the organization of the union defense guard in Minneapolis in 1938. We didn't say a word about anybody depriving the fascists of their right of free speech. We didn't say a word to the state or federal authorities about doing anything to prevent the fascists from speaking.

Our remarks were concentrated on explaining to the workers why they couldn't rely on any arm of the state apparatus to protect them against the fascists and why they should rely only on themselves to do so. It was along those lines that we set out to educate the members of Local 544 and the rest of the union movement.

How did the union defense guard go about this? Did we say we're not going to let the fascists speak and if they meet, we're going to break up their meeting? No. It wasn't us who said that. It was the Silver Shirts organizer. He said that in a statement that was quoted in the St. Paul press on the morning after they sneaked over to St. Paul and held a meeting, protected by the cops. They were afraid to have a meeting in Minneapolis. He said, the leaders of 544 say we can't have a meeting in Minneapolis.

That's what *he* said. What *we* said is that we're organizing a union defense guard and the guard is going to so conduct itself that it will show the fascists that they can't operate in Minneapolis without a fight. We just cut through this whole free speech business because that was not the crucial issue.

The issue is not for or against free speech for fascists. These people are not trying to promulgate an idea and convince somebody of a new line of thought in an academic way. They're organizing to commit acts of violence against others in order to destroy the fundamental rights of working people. They want to make the working people victims in a new and even worse form of this decaying capitalist system. There is nothing academic about that.

That's something we can seize on in explaining our antifascist struggle. In fact, you've got an even better case today than we had in 1938. The Silver Shirts only *said* they were going to make an armed raid on Local 544's hall. The fascist terrorists bombed the SWP twice in Los Angeles. It's a very peculiar form of friendly persuasion, isn't it? There's nothing academic about their objective in Los Angeles.

I'm talking now about how you combat the fatuous notions of professional civil libertarians and begin to intensify the education of students. If you put the struggle on the basis of whether the fascists have or don't have the right to speak, you create a real problem in trying to wake such forces up and mobilize them. We put our fight on the basis of what these fascists had said they were going to do—raid the union headquarters.

The essence of it then was to counterpose to the fascist actions the democratic right of a countermobilization. We bypassed the whole free speech question. Instead, we related intimately to that concrete situation by posing a second democratic right—the right of self-defense.

Keep in mind that the SWP was not a big organization at that time. However, it was not a question of the party stepping out to act against the fascists when there wasn't much to back it up. This was a union that had thousands of members.

Yet what did we do? You'll notice if you read *Teamster Politics* how careful we were to avoid giving any impression that this was a fight between 544 and the fascists, even though this union had a membership of thousands.

The situation was such that there could be no defense guard unless Local 544 took the initiative. We could not build a guard in a hurry that would be strong enough to repulse a Silver Shirt raid on the headquarters unless it was principally made up of 544 members. But we were not so foolish as to organize a 544 defense guard and confront the fascists on that basis. We wanted it to be the fight of the whole labor movement.

We thought it out tactically and used the device of setting up a provisional formation alongside the union. It wasn't an official part of the union. It was associated with the union only in the sense that its formation was discussed at a Local 544 membership meeting that voted to authorize the leadership to take the initiative in the name of 544 to set up a trade-union-wide defense guard.

At the same time that we were concentrating on organizing a guard big enough to be effective, concentrating principally on building it in 544, we were careful to set the stage for a wider body. Just as quickly as we could, we brought at least a few members of other unions into the guard. Nobody minded that this formation was called the 544 guard because the name 544 was kind of a mark of honor among the organized workers of Minneapolis, sort of like being part of the Grand Army of the Republic in the North after the Civil War. All it meant was that 544 had taken the initiative in organizing an antifascist defense within the Minneapolis trade union movement as a whole.

Local 544 not only took the initiative in building this trade-union defense formation, but held that the labor movement should organize all of labor's allies—the unemployed, the youth, and others. Right from the beginning, we projected the concept of acting in a united way and trying to develop an ever-broader united front of victims and potential victims of fascism, drawing them into the self-defense forces.

How did we organize the counter-demonstration? The Silver Shirts scheduled a meeting in Minneapolis. We knew what was on tap so we planned to send the guard to picket the hall where Pelley, the chieftain of the Silver Shirts, was scheduled to speak.

In *Teamster Politics* I described how on the appointed day a cab driver called Ray Rainbolt, a leader of the guard. The cabbie said he had just driven Pelley to a house in the silk-stocking district. That's the kind of intelligence system we had.

That is an important thing to realize about the working class. There isn't a nook or cranny of the capitalist machine where you won't find workers. Depending on the mood of the class, an individual worker who at one moment is a servitor of the ruling class, can at another moment become the eyes and ears of the workers in the camp of the enemy. When the struggle heats up, the working class develops the kind of spontaneous intelligence system that capitalist money can't buy.

Ray Rainbolt called Pelley and told him there might be trouble at the meeting. I didn't tell him to do that, he thought of it himself. Anything to keep the enemy worried, to give your forces an edge. Some people don't think these tactical niceties are so nice, but they're effective and perfectly principled. Rainbolt's idea was to scare the piss out of Pelley. Rainbolt was a good guy for this. He was a *mean* son of a gun. His ancestors were veterans of the clobbering of Custer and he hadn't lost the knack.

Here I'm getting at a concrete example of how the dynamics of a confrontation in the class struggle lead from one stage to another. We scared Pelley out of even going to the meeting. He decided against it. The minute the guard showed up the Silver Shirts began to take off like chickens in a barnyard, scampering this way and that. A few of them weren't fast enough and there were altercations that weren't entirely pleasant for the fascists.

We were not there formally or actually to prevent the fascists from speaking. We were there to show them that we were just as determined that they weren't going to carry out an attack on the trade unions as they were determined to carry one out—maybe more so. The question was not whether or not Pelley had the right to speak or whether these people had the right to come and hear him. We cut through that to the heart of the issue. Pelley was trying to organize forces to attack our headquarters and we were against that.

I have suggested that, instead of raising an attack on the formal democratic right of the fascists to speak and peddle their program and recruit goons, we counterpose the democratic right to counterdemonstrate. According to the tempo and development of the situation, we infuse into it the concept of the democratic right of self-defense.

Let's assume that a fascist is going to have a meeting. What kind of counterdemonstration are you going to have? What do you propose as the slogans or strategy of the demonstration? Are you going to rally on the site of the meeting? At UCLA [The University of California at Los Angeles], if they tried to send a Nazi goon on campus to exercise the right of free speech and to try to recruit, wouldn't an indicated theme of a counterdemonstration be the bombings of our headquarters?

If you have a counterdemonstration, this gives the government and its repressive arm no basis for moving toward real suppression of the democratic rights of the left in the name of evenhandedly suppressing both sides. On the contrary.

The police like to say that they're simply doing their duty under the constitution by protecting the fascists. Well, they are also duly sworn to protect the democratic rights of other Americans. One of the rights won in the class struggle is the right to picket, to hold counteractions. So you jockey the repressive forces so that, if they try to do something to help the fascists, it constitutes an overt and clear attack on the established democratic rights of the antifascists.

If you do that, the professional civil libertarians have no grounds for getting themselves worked up about how you are jeopardizing the Constitution by demanding the suppression of somebody's freedom of speech. Instead, you are in a good position to demand that the civil libertarians denounce the repressive forces that are using the phoney excuse of protecting the fascists' rights to justify violating the democratic right to counterdemonstrate.

If you do the opposite—make a big noise about how you're going to prevent the meeting, suppress the speaker—won't many students get confused and take the wrong stand? They don't want anybody to dictate to them who they can listen to, do they?

With the right approach, the students instead see a counterdemonstration outside the meeting. They see that the thrust is not on the right of the fascists to speak but on what they are actually doing in Los Angeles, for instance, to suppress our rights. Isn't that a favorable way to present it?

Starting from our initial premise—the aim of the capitalists with regard to fascism—I'm trying to look at each tactic from the point of view of its *effect*. What happens if you start out with the premise that you're going to organize a battle to prevent the fascists from saying one word in public? What happens, on the other hand, if you operate on the basis of asserting and exercising the right to counterdemonstrate, to confront the fascists in this form without getting bogged down in the question of the fascists' right of free speech? The first approach is to the advantage of the ruling class. The second approach puts you in a more favorable position and the ruling class in a more difficult position for carrying out its basic aim of crippling the rights of the antifascists.

To use a slight reformulation of that phrase of Malcolm X, the essence of the ruling class tactic toward oppositional movements like the struggle against fascism is to make the criminal appear to be the victim and the victim appear to be the criminal. They try that in every struggle, without exception. You always have to keep that in mind when you deal with the tactical nuances in the struggle.

Remember that tactics have to serve a strategic course, and the strategic course has to be closely attuned to the programmatic aims. It's not advantageous to grab hold of a tactic because it seems appealing at the moment without always seeing the tactic in relation to the whole fundamental problem.

Strategy is a system of tactics and something more as well. It contains the fundamental aim that you are moving toward. It is attuned to the conjunctural realities of the relationship of class forces and is readjusted as the relationship of class forces changes. Strategy is subject to variations in scope and tempo concerning the possible extent of its implementation. Simultaneously strategy is also the means by which you develop a system of tactics to serve your aims, and the regulator concerning the fundamental course that you follow in seeking to build the anticapitalist movement. It's always very important to see the struggle against fascism not only in its tactical aspect, but in its relationship to strategy and program.

Do you stop with a counterdemonstration against the fascists? No, but conceptually we start with it. What are the stages of struggle if we organize a protest confrontation against a fascist meeting? The first thing you can do, depending on the situation, is to alert those who go into the meeting that there's more going on than meets the eye in what the fascists have to say. You alert those going in the meeting or who observe the demonstration that the fascists are so dangerous that a lot of people are concerned about it. These people have gathered in front of the meeting hall to warn people that they're getting sucked into a trap, something that's against their own interests.

You don't start on the basis of the party confronting the Nazis. You try to muster the broadest forces possible. No matter what you do in any area, you draw on everybody you can.

There are two sides to that. The building of the broadest possible united front becomes an effective mechanism for educating the masses about the fascist danger. It creates the potential for drawing in ever-greater masses to confront the fascists. The more actively and consistently you apply this, the more difficult it is for the police forces to attack the antifascists and violate their democratic right to demonstrate against the fascists. You start on that basis and the action develops according to the interplay of forces.

Does that mean that it's always going to be that way? That the fascists will always be speaking inside and a counterdemonstration will always be outside and that's that? No, at a certain point the situation changes. There are several reasons why this is the case.

First of all, the fascists have a basic task to perform. They are trying to mobilize confused and demoralized victims of the capitalist system. One of the things they've got to show potential recruits is audacity. That causes them to lean in the direction of provocation.

Moreover, they know the cops are on their side and this makes them still more provocative. It's not as if one day, instead of a counterdemonstration, you take your forces and give the fascists a taste of their own medicine. It's not a question of on what date this can be done; the fascists also set the stage so that other things happen.

Don't forget Lenin and Trotsky made a revolution under defensive slogans. If you are obliged to clobber some fascist in order to protect your rights, it's always good if this is done in the name of defending yourself. It helps you to involve more allies. The fascists tend to be provocative and thus bring the situation past the stage of a counterdemonstration.

You start out on a realistic basis that gives the fascists no chance to fool people into thinking that you are violating democratic rights. This helps you to mobilize young people and win over civil libertarians. You build up the forces that will be able to deal with the fascists when the reality of the conflict between fascists and anti-fascists manifests itself in a more physical form.

One final point. Don't get the notion that you're facing the future fascist enemy when you face kooks like the Nazis or even the Klan. Don't get that notion for a minute. That's not the kind of animal we're talking about. In fighting against these screwballs today, keep in mind that you are shaping a strategic line and a set of tactics to face something that will be much different, much more sophisticated and even appealing to some, and not so easy to cope with.

There are two errors you can fall into if you don't keep this in mind. If you develop tactics based on the expectation that you're going to be facing this lunatic fringe, you'll find that you have the wrong strategic and tactical weapons in hand when you face the real thing. You can also obstruct the education of the masses about the threat of fascism because you alert the masses to the wrong creature. You get them on the lookout for monkeys when an elephant is going to charge them.

When the real thing comes along, it's not going to extend you the courtesy of being obvious like the Nazis in Los Angeles. They're not going to *start* by throwing bombs at you so that you can mobilize against them before they have a following. They are going to be more subtle.

They will claim that they are going to lead the masses out of the crisis created by capitalism. They will act in the name of promises that the masses believe will improve their desperate situation. They are going to pin the blame for the crisis on scapegoats. In this country, the Blacks are the most obvious target. By demagogically promising to do things for the people that they have no intention of doing, and by singling out scapegoats, the fascists aim to lead a demoralized and disoriented middle class, segments of the working class, and the lumpenproletariat to crush the organizations of the working class. Their fundamental aim will be to use some of the victims of capitalism to mobilize a force to crush the struggle capacity of the working class and perpetuate capitalist rule.

When you run up against the real thing, they're not going to start by putting on Nazi uniforms and swastika emblems, and they're not going to wear sheets, either. They'll look more like the man in the gray flannel suit than the ultraright we see today.

The capitalists are very happy to use the far-out types we run into today. They cause some confusion, stir things up a little, and plow a little ground for a more serious development of fascism. But they are not the real animal we will be fighting when the combat gets really tough.

STEVE CLARK: The concrete incident that led Ginny Hildebrand and I to want this discussion occurred at San Francisco State University. A professor invited a Nazi onto the campus to address his speech class on March 10, 1975. No right-wing student or faculty group was involved. In fact, the professor was known to have left-liberal leanings. The way he conducted his class was to bring in all kinds of professional speakers—preachers, Communists, and in this case a Nazi.

A demonstration was called with the stated aim of running this Nazi off campus and preventing his appearance before the class. It was called by the Spartacus Youth League, which describes itself as the youth section of the Spartacist League. The Progressive Labor Party and the Revolutionary Student Brigade were involved in one way or another on the same basic line. The real organizations with influence on campus—the Chicano student organization, the Black students organization, the women's organization, and some others that were approached—didn't want anything to do with the action.

The Young Socialist Alliance [YSA] refused to support or endorse this demonstration because of the way it was projected. We were aware of some of the basic ideas that Farrell laid out. We had learned the dangers of the confrontationist approach in the antiwar movement.

Until recently, there was some confusion in the YSA on the question of asking the government to ban fascist organizations, but we cleared this up. We incorporated the correct position on this into the Black struggle report that was adopted by the July 1974 Plenum of our National Committee.

In the same plenum report, however, we took a different tack than that proposed by Farrell on the question of the rights of Jensen, Shockley, the other academic racists, and, by implication, the fascists. We incorporated a lot of the lessons Farrell discussed. We opposed calling on the administration or the government to ban speakers. We thought we were avoiding the trap of placing the axis on freedom of speech, by avoiding actions like shouting the speakers down and other things which have led to unnecessary victimization of antiracists. But we said that the YSA does not believe racists and Nazis have the right to speak on campus.

After the National Committee approved this report, we published an article in the December 1974 issue of the *Young Socialist* [monthly newspaper of the YSA] about a demonstration against a Ku Klux Klan leader that spoke on a campus in St. Cloud, Minnesota. We thought the article would be useful for orienting the YSA membership about the kind of stand that should be taken.

Among other things, we really didn't differentiate clearly in this article between organizations like the KKK or the Nazis on the one hand, and racist academicians like Shockley on the other hand. We tended to lump them together.

In this situation in San Francisco, I think that 95 percent of what the YSA did was quite good. The YSA was clearly seen by the students as the one socialist group on campus that did not get caught up in this ultraleft attempt to keep a Nazi away from a speech class.

The Nazis only sent a few of their uniformed goons to the campus. It was easy, of course, for a few dozen students to chase them out. That is what happened. The Spartacists, Progressive Labor et al. considered this a very successful action because they had succeeded in doing what they set out to do. They did prevent this guy from speaking in that classroom. A historic triumph in the struggle against fascism, in their view.

This made the front page of the San Francisco *Chronicle,* the big daily out there, and there was a great deal of alarm on the campus that a small group had taken upon itself to decide who could speak. The administration used it to whip up a little campaign against the student movement.

So the YSA at San Francisco State issued a statement which was right on the essential points. However, it repeated what had appeared in this

1974 YSA National Committee plenum report. It argued that, although the YSA opposed the fascist's appearance on campus, we were opposed to preventing him from speaking unless a majority were educated to approve this course. We criticized the ultraleft action. Of course, we stated our opposition to any disciplinary measures against the students who had participated in this adventure.

At that point, Bob Chester and some of the leaders of the SWP branch in San Francisco expressed doubts to the YSA leadership about whether it was correct to advocate suppression of free speech at all, even conditionally. Bob Chester gave some classes on fascism and how to fight it, laying out his view on this.

That convinced the YSA organizer who wrote a letter and asked me whether the position taken by Bob and others there stood in contradiction to the line of the YSA plenum report. It seemed to me that there was a contradiction. I wanted to consult with some more experienced comrades on this matter and that was the genesis of this meeting.

Right now there is a defense case at San Francisco State because the administration did just what Farrell said they would do in such circumstances. They took pictures of the students that were involved and now they are trying to victimize the organizations that demonstrated.

The Nazis are talking about coming back on campus sometime in the near future. They put out a leaflet with all kinds of racist epithets and drawings that says roughly: "Free Speech? These radicals who talk to you about free speech are trying to tell you who to listen to and what to think. Are you going to take that?" So they're trying to get a little mileage out of the exposed position the ultralefts put themselves in.

The Spartacists and some others have set up a March 10 Defense Committee to oppose administration reprisals. Unfortunately, we haven't really been able to participate in this committee since it demands that we support the ultraleft action as a precondition for united front defense. But we are doing our own defense work, mainly propaganda. We've put out a second leaflet opposing any victimizations. We see the outcome of this case as being important for the whole student movement on campus. The outcome is up in the air at this point. In the course of our propaganda, it is necessary for us to have a clear position. On campus, the general impression of the YSA is that we are not opposed to free speech.

At the upcoming plenum of the YSA National Committee, we will begin a process of discussion in the YSA to clarify some of these questions. Farrell's comments have convinced me that the formulation we used in the 1974 plenum report is a bad one. It's basically self-contradictory to say that we don't call upon the state or campus administration to ban these fascist groups and at the same time say that they have no right to speak.

That's a stand that legitimizes state repression even if it is hedged in by statements that oppose capitalist state repression of fascists. The formulation provides cover for capitalist repression even if, as we did, you insist on mass action with majority support. Of course, it legitimizes it even more when you propose repression by small groups of radicals as the alternative to state repression, as the Spartacus Youth League and the others did. I think we will have to straighten out this contradiction in our position at the next plenum.

A more knotty question is our attitude to racist professors and geneticists like Shockley, Jensen, Herrnstein, and others who are going on speaking tours of the campuses to promulgate racist theories. We've tended to say the same thing about them that we said about the Nazis.

The way we tried to keep the issue off the free speech axis was to say that these people claim to be exercising free speech, but that's not the issue. Their racist theories simply bolster attacks on Black people by the KKK, ROAR, and the rest. Their speeches are not just talk but inspirations to racist violence and racial discrimination. At the same time, we've also opposed confrontationist actions that put activists in needless danger. I now think we've been wrong in opposing in our propaganda the "right" of these people to speak on campus.

There is another problem related to the previous ones. We in the YSA more or less raised refusal to debate Shockley to the level of a principle. On the other hand, we unhesitatingly seek out the most rabid Zionists—who are every bit as racist—for debates. That's because there is such a small anti-Zionist audience and it helps expose the Zionist position. It attracts uncommitted people who want to hear a confrontation of views on the Middle East.

Whenever Shockley comes to campus, several wings shape up in the meetings that prepare the antiracist response. There is a wing that says stop him at all costs and the mood of the campus be damned. Then there's another wing that argues that the best thing we can do is try to turn this meeting into a debate.

They propose that we should get some professor who is a competent geneticist or, even better, an antiracist activist who knows his stuff in this area and debate Shockley. Then you have the contention of ideas before the students rather than letting them simply be saturated with Shockley's racist pseudo-science inside the hall while all we have is a few slogans outside.

Thus far the YSA has said, "No. This only helps to build the meetings. We shouldn't dignify these racist views by debating them."

I've begun to have some doubts whether this was a wise stance for us to take. These racists are coming on with pseudoscientific arguments and some students listen and take it for good coin.

It's a tactical issue with a strong emotional impact associated with it. We debate all sorts of people on all sorts of questions. In my opinion, we based our "no debate" tactic on the emotional intensity of the issue. As I said, I'm beginning to think the YSA was tactically wrong on some of these things.

JACK BARNES: It is fortunate that this is coming up now. It will make it much easier to educate people on these questions.

There are several problems that are closely linked to the points made in Farrell's presentation. I think one of the problems is the middle-class view of the campus that is unconsciously held by a lot of people in the radical movement. They think of the campus as some kind of unsullied sea of reasoned discourse that is somehow different from the rest of society. One reason why we are opponents of student power strategies and proponents of the red university strategy is because we recognize that the university is deeply interlinked with class society. The processes going on in society, including class polarization, reflect themselves on campus. Let's begin with that reality, and then we can fit all our strategy and tactics on campus into the broader strategy and tactics of the class struggle.

That's why I think Farrell was right to begin where he did. We don't start with the Constitution, or the Bill of Rights, or the fascists. We start with the preparation of our class and its vanguard for the coming struggles. That's the axis that everything we do revolves around.

This idea of the special character of the campus plays into the hands of the right-wing liberals and professional civil-libertarians who want to pretend that there's some way to keep class polarization away from the campus. Some say let the Nazis go out to a white working-class neighborhood and talk to those racist workers, but not on our campus. There's a lot of that. It's middle-class.

It also plays into the hands of the ultralefts who think there are different rules for combat on campus than exist somewhere else.

With this outlook, the YSA's concept of the red university and the student movement will be seen in a new light and a new facet will come to view. We have to drive home this idea of the class polarization and its reflection on the campus.

Over the next ten or fifteen years, many of your fascist-minded speakers on campus are going to have tenure. They're not going to be outsiders or guys wearing German SS uniforms. There are going to be fascist professors and teaching assistants. Some of them will be effective organizers and ideologues and spokespersons for a genuine fascist movement.

This correct view of the campus, our strategy, and the role of the fascists within it, will differentiate us from the liberals and the ultralefts. It will help our cothinkers around the world. This problem is even less understood in other countries where there are real traditions of university autonomy. Police aren't supposed to set foot on the campus. Of course, whenever social tension is high, all that goes by the boards.

What is the problem that our comrades really face in their day to day work? A major one is ultraleft pressure. They have to handle the ultraleft arguments of the Maoists, the new left remnants, the Marcyites, the Workers League, the Spartacists, etc. Every campus must have four or five of these groups—ultraleft student groups, ultraleft organizations of the oppressed nationalities, ultraleft feminists, etc.

The pressure comes because our people hate the fascists and the right wing and so do these people. It's like a discussion within the movement, not outside it. Our people don't bend to the civil libertarians, to the Republican and Democratic politicians, but on this point they were bending to ultraleftism.

I think one thing we have to do is put the whole question of fascism into proper proportion. The main approach to fighting these people today is as *racists*, not as fascists. Fascism is not an imminent threat in the United States, but the mobilization of racist forces is.

The racist offensive is not only an imminent threat but a gigantic campaign that has been organized and mobilized for over a decade by the ruling class. Showdowns with real social forces are taking place over education, jobs, housing, from Milwaukee to Boston to Los Angeles to Chicago to Houston to Baltimore.

I would think that the axis for the mobilization of broad forces—not just a few ultralefts—would be to concentrate on the racist aspect. Racist mobilizations, racist theories, racist opinions, and racist agitators are part of this attempt to build up a racist offensive. They show the need for a counteroffensive. That should be the stress in our statements. When it would be accurate to say so, we can also point out that these people are fascists and what that means.

I was impressed by a story Steve Chainey, the SWP organizer in San Francisco, told me about a probusing demonstration held by the National Student Coalition Against Racism. It was attended by a significant number of Blacks, students, and youth. Black youth made up a large part of the defense guard. The Nazis came up in their truck with their storm troopers uniforms and a sound system. They started a racist harangue. Of course, the first reaction of people on the demonstration was to throw taunts back at them.

The marshals had a discussion and they recognized that this Nazi display was a provocation. Its objective role was to direct attention away from the real enemy, the segregationist Boston school board, the rulers in Boston, and their backers in the White House. The effect of a confrontation with the Nazis would be to focus attention instead on these ten nuts in a halftrack. The papers would report that a bunch of us beat up ten of them or they beat up some of us, instead of having to report about a thousand people mobilized against the racist school board.

So the marchers just ignored the Nazis and drove ahead with the rally. You start with the struggle against racism and the practical needs of that struggle. That makes sense to a serious Black militant or a serious worker or student. The ultralefts, of course, don't see it that way. In their view, you are obliged to drop everything, throw all other issues to the side, and start showing this little bunch of Nazis how rough and tough you are.

You might want to consider including some comments in the report you are preparing for the YSA plenum on the National Caucus of Labor Committees. While none of these little fascist groups of today are like the real critter that is going to come down the road, there are more aspects of it in the NCLC (or "U.S. Labor Party" as it sometimes styles itself) than in the Nazis.

Here you have people who attack the union movement, the Black movement, and radical groups of all stripes. They have goon squads. They orient toward the lumpen proletariat, the cops, and toward sectors of students and middle-class radicals who are shaken up by the growth of the crisis and are looking for answers. The axis of their presentation is the road for the masses out of the crisis produced by the "Rockefeller-CIA conspiracy."

They put out newspapers and magazines that campaign on this, claiming that they are for a radical solution in the interest of the masses. They have people in some of the unions and they carry out radical-sounding antilabor propaganda among the workers. The labor movement has more problems with the NCLC than with the Nazis. They cause more confusion, because people think of them as radical or even communist rather than reactionary. The same was true of the real Nazis, the German ones. While I don't predict that the NCLC is likely to become a mass organization, it is a better example of the more serious and complicated aspects of fascism than the American Nazis.

I think the YSA's only mistake was the one statement opposing the fascists' right to speak on the campus. That was unnecessary. In one sense, of course, these murdering goons have no right to breathe air. But that sentence could be interpreted as meaning that radical groups are taking it upon themselves to decide that these individuals have no Bill of Rights protection. We don't say that.

I think too much credence is given in the *Young Socialist* to the idea that the big goal is to stop the racists from speaking—if not now, then later. I noticed that the last line in the *Young Socialist* article on the antiracist demonstration in Minnesota states that while it didn't stop the head of the Klan from speaking, it did begin to educate. This gives people the wrong impression of our objectives. If it really did begin to educate and mobilize, then that's the important thing—and not whether you stopped one fascist from talking for an hour on one campus.

The structure of the passage gives your cadres the wrong impression that the number one goal was to stop him, but it was premature to carry that out. It's going to be necessary to stop fascist forces one day, but they will not be a direct outgrowth of this individual. Whether he speaks or not is not what will decide the future struggle between racism and antiracism, or fascism and antifascism. The key thing is how you mobilize, organize, and politically arm and prepare the mass forces that are going to have to do the stopping. What you *did* in Minnesota was very good in that regard.

The YSA organizer in San Francisco wrote in her letter that our approach has to be firmed up because we are going to confront this problem frequently if we are successful in helping to organize a strong antiracist movement. For instance, if a fighting youth organization for desegregation develops, or if the NAACP or other forces move in the direction of taking on the racist forces, the whole antiracist movement will be continually confronted with these problems.

All kinds of people will want the antiracist movement to spearhead premature efforts to stop the racists or bust up a Nazi meeting, or tear out the telephone in the house where Chicago's racist hotline is quartered. That's because the people we work with will have a healthy hatred for these racist scum and will size them up for what they are, the spearhead of a national racist offensive. With that in mind, the report that is given to the YSA plenum should be understandable not only to your National Committee, but to antiracist activists all over the country.

Tactically, you have to differentiate between Shockley and the Nazis. There is a whole spectrum of outright fascists, right-wing professors, right-wing students, secretly right-wing types, open racist elements, secretly racist elements, groups that favor a stronger role for the military, etc. You have to be aware of the qualitative differences between some of these shades as well as the breadth of the spectrum. You handle each type slightly differently.

At the point where we are in the evolution of class consciousness in this country, and the state of the student movement in relation to that overall level of class consciousness, you cannot deal with Shockley or Jensen exactly as you would deal with fascists.

On these questions we have the job of winning the minds not only of the masses but of the vanguard. Even many of the more capable students cannot self-confidently explain what's wrong with these theories. You've got to take them on at that theoretical level, as well as on the level of the implicit politics of what Jensen and Shockley are doing. It will be greatly appreciated in the Black community if forces come forward to rebut this racist fakery in plain language, cogently and scientifically. On this question, one of our weapons is science.

Of course, we don't invite these people to campus, but we also know that they are going to be on campus. There are going to be debates and people are going to go to them and a lot of racists are going to look to these pseudoscientists for ammunition. The young militants will want to know how to rebut the Jensens. They really appreciate it when you give them ammunition, answer their questions, clarify their confusions so that they can answer the questions of others in their milieu. We should mobilize some of our better young minds that have experience and knowledge in science, genetics, and history and provide people with the whole picture of why they're wrong. Then the main support the right-wingers will have on this point will be the hard-core racists and fascists.

You can't laugh off these racist theoreticians. On

the question of debating racists, there is an important thing to keep in mind. The fascists *educated* millions on theories of racial superiority and inferiority. They didn't just appeal to emotions and use violence and mass psychology. They also educated on the basis of their racial myths. They had books and textbooks and they made use of the rising film industry. People went around and lectured, showing alleged skulls of Jews and jawbones of Blacks and claiming to prove scientific points with them. They talked learnedly about migrations and where the different races came from. It was all pseudo-scientific claptrap, of course.

In many cases, the fascist leaders were completely cynical about their own ideologies. That was just bait for suckers. But the people they appealed to were not always cynical about the Nazi ideology. In the context of a social crisis, these ideas were a recruiting tool. The fascists recognized that, among other things, you have to win over the minds of the people and give them the rudiments of explanations that seem to be in line with reality to the listeners.

So we can't just ignore these ideologists. We have the duty to provide counterinformation to the racist propaganda, and there should be no embarrassment about doing it. We have to get the *Militant* and the *Young Socialist* involved in this process.

The emotional reaction against such debates is natural. Black people know they are not genetically inferior to whites. They are in a better position than anybody to know white people as they really are. They have no illusions on that score.

But, if they think it out they are going to see that the battle is to win the minds of the masses in this country. There is nothing more popular in the Black community than a speaker who can give a wonderful talk on Black history. Malcolm X was one example. Black people know they have a great history. But when someone articulates it, inspires people by it, there is tremendous appreciation for that in the Black community. They will feel the same way about militants who can go into a debate and tear these racists apart with the facts, and the political explanations that underlie the facts.

Progressive-minded people are open to thinking scientifically, thinking materialistically, and thinking dialectically. They appreciate this kind of education and it arms them and inspires them.

The ultralefts are thinking about street-fighting tactics. But we are arming people with the ideas they will need over the long haul. That way we will come out ahead not only today, but in the real street fighting that history tells us is going to take place in a profound social crisis.

GINNY HILDEBRAND: I have a couple of questions regarding very specific situations. I agree with Jack and Farrell completely about getting off the axes of free speech and preventing the meetings. We have opposed confrontations.

We have said concerning Shockley and Jensen that their theories are aimed at dehumanizing Blacks, etc. When these people come to campus, we make use of that move on their part to spur on a movement that is counter to the racists. We also put forward demands around whatever specific antiracist struggles are going on at the time.

We also point out that Shockley and Jensen represent certain fringes of the racist movement, and that the Nazis and the Klan represent in a certain sense its ultimate logic.

One thing I have a question about is how we use this term "rights." If one of these racists comes on campus and we're having a counterdemonstration and a reporter comes up and asks, "Do you think fascists or racists have the right to speak," we take the approach that this is not the issue.

But if you are in a planning meeting before a demonstration against a Nazi or a Jensen, it isn't only the sectarians who place the axis on barring these people from speaking. You have a lot of serious students, including Black students, who feel the same way that we do, that these purveyors of racist violence don't have any right to do this.

What we want to do in that situation, I would think, is strategically explain the tactical approach that needs to be taken. But when this question comes up, don't you have to identify with the sentiment that they don't have the right to speak, and then explain that this is not the real issue? Shouldn't we say that even though others will pick it up and use it in an ultraleft way? What should we say in such meetings to avoid either being misunderstood or encouraging harmful adventures?

There is one thing that can't be stressed enough that I know we are all in agreement on. The struggles on the campuses have in large part revolved around this question of opposing free speech for racists. We will often be in a situation where an ultraleft tendency or a student group that has a different orientation from our own gets the jump on us in organizing against some racist speaker. They begin to organize a demonstration with slogans against the right of free speech and possibly even set the goal of breaking up the meeting. I think that we should not simply abstain, even though we may not be able to participate in this or that action. I think comrades should be aggressive about carrying out educational work against the racists or even helping to initiate another demonstration on a more realistic basis. We have to be active in this struggle even if some forces are a little bit off the track at times.

Finally, how in general do we go about defending people who do engage in adventurist confrontations against the Nazis and the racist academicians? They've gotten themselves into a spot where their intentions can be misunderstood, where they don't appear to be defending themselves against the racists but to be attacking the racists, and they've isolated themselves somewhat. What's the best approach to take in defending them?

Dobbs: There's one aspect raised by the ultraleft action in San Francisco State that is particularly interesting. How do you go about defending them against the measures taken against them by the authorities?

This can be used to drive home a lesson that has a very deep thrust and wide application. You don't put it on the axis of apologizing for them by saying they did something wrong, but they shouldn't be victimized. You can use the attack on these ultralefts to show the students that, in the confrontations with fascism, the government—in this case, the university administration—is on the fascists' side and against the antifascists. In San Francisco, the ruling authorities are trying to punish people who prevented a fascist from speaking. In Los Angeles, their counterparts in the ruling structure can't seem to find the right-wing terrorists that bombed our headquarters. The San Francisco comrades might find similar examples closer to home. That way you can turn a negative, a tactical disadvantage, into a positive, a tactical advantage.

Never approach these situations on the basis simply of the narrow factors involved in the specific situation. Don't think of it in terms of defending people who got victimized by the ruling class because they carried out an incorrect line. Approach it from the angle of how are we going to turn that against the capitalists. When you are thinking about tactics, place every episode into the larger picture of your strategy and objectives. To view the episode only in isolation is a mistake.

Once you do that, two things immediately suggest themselves here. One, these people got caught in a bind. They demonstrated in life the foolishness of trying to substitute themselves for the masses in trying to put a stop to the fascist efforts to recruit on the campuses. The other side of it is that they are being clobbered by a government that isn't doing a damn thing when the fascists violate the right of free speech for other people. They even look the other way when these forces commit crimes that come within the definition of attempted murder. The attack on the authorities in this instance focuses on the discriminatory policies of the government in the confrontation between the fascists and the antifascists.

One of the key problems for a tactician is to think out ways to turn negatives into positives. It's natural to feel, "Jesus Christ, we could have done without this! If it isn't our enemies who create problems for us, we've got to watch out for those who say they want the same things we do."

It's better to say, "Okay, the ultralefts botched it. Now how can we take this situation and turn it against the enemy and even make the ultralefts useful in spite of themselves."

Let me add a little fillip to Jack's description of the San Francisco parade in solidarity with the Black students in Boston. SWP and YSA members weren't the entire monitoring force, of course, but they played a significant part.

Not only did the monitors interpose themselves between the marchers and the Nazis, but they deliberately and demonstratively formed a line with their backs to the Nazis. I liked that little note. It was a very effective way of silently signaling to the marchers, don't let these Nazis divert us from our purpose. Don't let them screw up our demonstration as they would so very much like to do. Masses understand such silent signals. I like that kind of thinking. Knowing how to do such little things makes a skillful tactician. When you find someone who is capable of thinking fast and acting accordingly in matters of this kind, you've got the makings of a tactician.

Clark: It's not just sectarians and ultralefts who have these emotional responses to the idea of allowing Nazis to speak or debating Shockley and Jensen. There are Black students and Black student organizations that react to these racists by wanting to take action to stop them here and now.

It isn't just a question of Black students who are organized into political tendencies either, although this is part of what the Young Socialist Alliance members confront. The point Jack made about pressure from the ultraleft has validity but it is not primarily an ideological problem.

In dealing with the question of how to fight the Nazis at San Francisco State, for instance, we had the problem of differentiating ourselves from the Spartacus Youth League without appearing to be siding just a little bit with the Nazis, without appearing to be soft. These sectarian groups have orators who will try very hard to whip up a frenzy on this theme and sometimes this will have an impact on militant Black students, although this was not at all the case at San Francisco State.

In the case of a Shockley meeting, a similar problem arises. How do you take a stand in favor of debate, for instance, when these Black students just hate the guts of these racists and for very good reason. Many of these Black students don't have any civil-libertarian hangups. They just have a gut hatred for these racists that sometimes blinds them to the tactical considerations Farrell and Jack have raised. How do you deal with sentiment of this kind in a Black student organization, for instance.

That's a source of the pressure the YSA faces. It's not the broad student milieu that is the source of this pressure. The average student is almost always confused by this free speech issue, as Farrell said. But it isn't the sectarian groups that are the main source of pressure, either.

When we participate in a united front demonstration against Shockley, these Black students are bitterly outraged by him. A couple of them will sometimes go into the meeting and hear what this guy is spewing out. They bring it back to the demonstrators. Several times the picket-line monitors have lost control of the demonstrations because of this. Fifty or sixty Black students just went inside and started shouting down the racist. These are often very large meetings and the relationship of forces is against them. The result is that the Black students get victimized. This happened at Yale, for instance.

To the extent that our members may be uncomfortable with the educational process that we have to carry out on this issue, I think that the problem will not be how do we answer the Spartacist League, but how do we present our arguments to people like those Black students at Yale.

Barnes: The problem is ultraleftism. In this case, it is ultraleftism on the part of Black students.

It is understandable ultraleftism. They hate the racists who deny their rights and their humanity. The source of the ultraleftism of the Spartacists is also their antipathy to racism, capitalism, fascism, and all the other evils of society. They are also individuals who believe they hate the racists and the right. They also have gut reactions.

You can begin with an entirely justified gut reaction, but its reflection on the level of tactics, strategy, and action in these cases is ultraleftism. The ultralefts in the Black student movement don't know the time of day any more than the Spartacists. There's no difference on that level at all.

The worst disservice you can do to the Black liberation movement is to adapt to ultraleftism because of the color of the ultraleftist's skin. We don't adapt to class-collaborationism when Black Democrats run for office and we shouldn't adapt to ultraleftism in the Black liberation struggle either. In both cases, of course, we run into gut reactions that are different from our class-struggle position.

We give the same arguments to the Spartacists as to the Black students and vice versa. You have to begin with the time of day.

On some campuses you may be able to prevent these racists from being invited. Instead you may have a public meeting in the chapel paid for by the university and attended by thousands of students and faculty members. You may have a talk on the real origins of humanity, the real history of Black people, exposing the racist frauds. That's the best variant. That means the particular campus is at a certain political level and the relationship of forces is such that there's no base of support for the racists. You can transform that campus into an educational megaphone for science against racism and for mobilizing against racism—on and off the campus.

That's the best situation. At Yale or Duke University, to take two examples, the relationship of forces is not that good. The level of consciousness is not that high. It follows that Shockley will appear. If you physically try to break up the meeting, whether or not you succeed, you will be worse off for your efforts. You begin with the time of day, not with your gut. You use your head. Shockley is going to appear on a lot of campuses.

So what do you do? You size up the situation and figure out what's best. Maybe it's a picket line. Maybe it's to get the university to provide $3,000 for one of the Black students to articulate another point of view.

Steve noted that the leaders of an anti-Shockley demonstration at Yale that we were involved in lost control of the picket line. You lost control of that picket line because you broke a fundamental rule. You didn't think out your real goals and prepare beforehand to achieve them. The troops didn't fully comprehend why they were there and for what reason. If the political objective is presented, with whatever provisos and hesitations, as preventing the speech, then demonstrators are going to feel drawn toward doing that, and they will suffer setbacks accordingly. There has to be clarity on the political objectives. It's a good lesson to learn and I'm glad you were able to learn it with so few casualties. There will be more important picket lines in the future and the provocation is going to be much greater.

We had to take on ultraleftism in many of its forms in the antiwar movement. There were some ultraleft tendencies in the Black struggle that played a destructive role in the antiwar movement. We had to teach the entire movement how to deal with these things politically and we won over many Black militants in that way. It's a much worse disservice to pander or adapt to a wrong political concept that is coming from a serious Black militant than it is to give ground to a hardened sectarian, if you want to deal with differentiations of that kind. We have got to persuade people to transform their gut feelings, which we also have, into conscious strategies that can achieve the defeat of racism.

On defending groups that get caught up in adventures—somehow the victims of these adventures always turn out to be the demonstrators and almost never their intended targets—we have to take the cases as they come. Why does the administration victimize these students? Because the demonstrators were opposed to the fascists, that's why. In the course of defending them, you try in a nonsectarian way to get across the lesson of the outcome of their action. The logic of these situations is that if the radical students and the oppressed nationalities follow the ultralefts' lead, they'll all be off the campus sooner or later.

It's like walking into the administration office and saying, "We'd like you to get rid of the lot of us." The administration is happy to oblige. Let's defend the victims but let's also educate so there won't be any more victims.

If the Spartacists insist on setting up a defense committee that supports their adventurist actions, we can't be part of if. If they want us to sign a loyalty oath that we think their tactics are great, we will have to politely say "no." In that case, we do whatever is practical and useful to oppose the victimizations.

Doug Jenness: I would like to comment on Ginny's concern that comrades might be put on the spot if they came out for the right of fascists to come on the campus. It strikes me that comrades should not feel they have to make some kind of moral declaration that would put us in the position of conceding that such and such a group doesn't have any rights. It's a trap.

These are racists who are bombing Black people's homes and threatening Black school children. The issue is how to fight them. We have to figure out how to build the most effective and biggest protest against their violations of democratic rights.

Ultralefts accuse us of just wanting to educate. We certainly want to educate, but our proposals are also a more effective form of struggle. We aim at mobilizing the largest number of people with the least chance of victimization.

I would like to make one point on debating these racist geneticists. In general, you may find that it is better to have an antiracist militant debate one of these geneticists than a liberal professor, even one who has excellent knowledge of the scientific issues involved. Shockley and Jensen are pretty slick at giving a pseudoscientific form to what is essentially a political argument for keeping Black people at the bottom.

I've seen cases where one of these liberal professors would debate Jensen and get pretty badly mauled because they were less clear and consistent than Jensen on the *political* issues. They don't understand the real nature of racial oppression. They may stumble around and give ground where absolutely none should be given.

Often a Black militant who is a capable speaker will give a more effective presentation because he or she knows what racial oppression is and how it works. So it might be better to have an antiracist militant study the scientific aspects of the question and take on these racist theories from a more consistent political point of view than some of these well-meaning liberal academics can put forward.

GEORGE NOVACK: The basic position of the party on this question was formulated in a resolution on the capitalist witch-hunt adopted at the February 1950 Plenum of the SWP National Committee. It is reprinted in an Education for Socialists publication, *Defense Policies and Principles of the Socialist Workers Party*. [See also the Education for Socialists publication, *The Fight Against Fascism in the USA*.]

On the question that was posed about how to answer when we are asked whether or not racists or fascists have the right to speak on campus, my opinion is that this question has to be turned around.

Our concern as socialists and antiracists in this instance is not whether this individual or that individual has the right to speak. Our concern is the abuse of this right by the fascists and racists to rationalize and encourage taking away the rights of the masses of Black people, the abuse of this right to incite violence against Black people in Boston or elsewhere. Put the question in the proper framework and on the right axis.

This problem has to be seen in the light of our long-range tasks. There are three major sites of social struggle in this country—the factories, the communities of the oppressed nationalities and national minorities, and the campuses. The Young Socialist Alliance as a student organization has its attention focused on the campuses.

There are ten million college students and hundreds of thousands of faculty members in a country that is probably the oldest democratic republic in the world. People in this country are very sensitive about their democratic rights, and rising expectations have made them even more sensitive. That is why they can respond to attacks on our rights. We can't get ourselves into the position where we advocate the abrogation of anyone's democratic rights as such.

This country is divided into classes and the classes contend with each other. In this contest, we counter the meeting of fascists or racists on a campus with the demand for a countermobilization. Here you have the counterposition of democratic rights by two sides. The contending forces appeal to the same democratic rights, codified in the same bourgeois-democratic constitution. That is the ground on which the conflict initially and formally stands.

That is where the concrete realities of the class struggle come to the fore, sometimes leading to physical combat. If that happens, it is all part of the struggle. We don't go in for adventures and we don't encourage adventures. It's just that when opposing forces come to grips, fighting sometimes results. That is part of the process of determination of the relationship of forces on a campus, in a city, and in the nation.

We certainly want to be in a position where the relationship of forces is changed in favor of our class and its allies. We want the fascists, racists, and sexists to feel intimidated and afraid of doing their dirty work. But we don't want this to take the form of restrictions on democratic rights, because that can lead to restrictions on our advocacy or that of any progressive force.

We do what we have to do without indulging in orations against anyone's democratic rights.

HILDEBRAND: This discussion has clarified my thinking on how to proceed and on what line should be taken to the YSA plenum to begin the educational process on this question. By presenting the whole issue in this perspective, we should be able to clarify a lot of things for the YSA members.

BETSEY STONE: The activity of these fascist groups is alarming a lot of people in the Black community and they want to do something about it. The first reaction is very emotional because these fascists are challenging the very right of a people to live. But the Black community is very interested in and ready to listen to practical and effective ways of combating these forces.

When we talk about this issue, it is always from the point of view of hatred for these fascist forces and the perspective of destroying them. The ultralefts want to debate about free speech. The Nazis figure they have nothing to lose from this. That's just falling into their trap.

FARRELL DOBBS: One point, specifically on the right of free speech. We don't fight for free speech for Nazis. We defend the right of free speech against the fascists and against the government, and we don't want to hand them any weapons for suppressing our free speech.

We don't advocate free speech for Nazis the way the professional civil libertarians do. We don't view it as a concept that rises above the laws of the class struggle.

Our aim is to crush the fascists. That aim is dictated by their nature and the methods they use against our class. The civil libertarians may dream that this conflict will be resolved by polite exchanges of views. The struggle with fascism won't be settled that way. Either the workers are going to crush the fascists or the fascists will crush the workers.

We stand in opposition to the government trying to put restrictions on the Nazis, because they turn any such restrictions against our class and its allies. We stood in opposition to the government of New York City in 1961 when it tried to prevent the American Nazi leader Rockwell from speaking in Union Square [see *The Fight Against Fascism in the USA*].

If we had kept silent or supported the government's action in that instance, we would have been helping the government set a precedent for use against the next four or five civil rights or peace actions. We don't make speeches against free speech for anybody because of the same kind of considerations. But we are under no illusions that the fight with the fascist groups will be settled by speech.

It's a coldblooded tactical proposition. A lot of people are already in our party and I hope an infinite number are yet to come. As people mostly born and bred in the USA, they will come around us with all the thinking habits of American pragmatism and formal logic. They may think that since the SWP doesn't call for the suppression of free speech in the case of fascists, therefore the SWP is interested in the fascists' right to speak.

No. Our concern is with the rights of our class and its allies. It's in the nature of things that our rights and the rights of the labor movement and the Black movement will collide with the supposed rights of the fascists—because the fascists view their rights as a license to kill, a license to crush the workers' movement.

Secondly, when you talk about the fight against fascism, you are talking about combat. The object of the ruling class in trying to build a fascist movement is to prepare, alongside the institutions of parliamentary rule, extraparliamentary forces to crush the working class and its allies and lay the basis for capitalism to impose a very brutal form of dictatorship. Between now and the time that showdown comes—and it's going to come, that's a law of history—the ruling class will resort to every possible means including the most bloody violence to perpetuate its power and its privileges.

The ruling class always comes to the point where it seeks to pass from bourgeois democracy through interim stages like Bonapartism or military dictatorship to fascism. The whole period between now and then is one of mobilizations and countermobilizations leading to the final showdown. Viewed in that perspective, mobilizing forces for self-defense against the extraparliamentary attacks of the fascists can be seen as a step in a process that leads to the formation at a certain stage of a working-class army like the army that the Bolsheviks forged in Russia after they came to power.

The line-up in the preliminary stage is one of the ruling class attempting to mobilize initial fascist forces. The conscious revolutionary vanguard has the task of mobilizing the forces that are going to prevent the fascists from imposing their dictatorship in the crunch. That crunch occurs later when we're at a higher, more intensive stage of struggle, when the capitalist crisis has become far deeper than today.

If you start by attempting to hastily gather together a vanguard force and crush fascism in the egg, you are playing into the hands of the fascists. You are losing ground in the mobilization of the real class that can do away with fascism, and the fascists are gaining ground as a result. Now that's the problem the ultralefts fell into in San Francisco.

With a new wave of the current radicalization, we will witness the beginning of a process that was characterized by the appearance of a diversity of phenomena in the thirties. On the one side there was the German American Bund or the Silver Shirts, counterparts at that time of the Klan and the Nazis.

On the other hand, we had Coughlin. He was a somewhat different animal. Frank Hague, the mayor of Jersey City, was yet a different animal. Study that period in this respect, with all its nuances.

Until Roosevelt, the Stalinists, the Social Democrats, and the old-line union hacks like Tobin succeeded in blocking the political radicalization of the class, the ruling class was terrified that they might see a revolutionary explosion. It was no accident that the first signs of an incipient fascist development began in the early 1930s. Pelley started the Silver Shirts in 1932.

It was also no accident that the right-wing polarization began to take a more serious form when it appeared in the late 1930s that the labor radicalization had been stalled. Confusion was created by the failure of the working-class to respond independently to the new depression of 1937–1938. This was no little economic dip but a very severe slump. In those circumstances Coughlin and Hague, the serious fascists, were able to enter a confused political scene that resulted from the crisis of working-class leadership. The fascist danger was not washed out by anything the labor leadership did, but only when the path followed by the ruling class led into World War II. Then all the ground rules changed.

What has happened since then? A long period of cold war and witch-hunt transpired, with economic stability and quiescence in the class struggle. Things began to change with the turn in the Black struggle in the 1950s, the student radicalization, women's struggles, and the antiwar movement. With the new economic depression and the beginning of new thinking in the working class, you are seeing new signs of incipient fascism interrelated with the repressive actions of the government.

You are going to see the rise of counterparts of Hague and Coughlin—in a different form, in different garb, but a comparable type. Remember, you've now got a more desperate ruling class that had to haul its ass out of Saigon in a hurry. The imperialists scrambled out with their tails between their legs the way the special deputies left the market in the 1934 Minneapolis strike.

BARNES: As a military tactician, you must have appreciated that skillful retreat.

DOBBS: I loved every minute of it.

As I was saying, we have to see the next period as a period of mobilization of fascist forces and countermobilization of working-class forces. That is the context in which we develop our tactics. Someone who begins with the concept that you can defeat the enemy without a major battle is making a big error. There is going to be a battle, a direct confrontation with whatever forces the capitalist class can muster to perpetuate its rule. Don't go out with a corporal's guard thinking that if you can smash a few scouts on the other side, the real enemy army will cut and run and never take to the field of battle. You've got to meet them power to power.

Tactically, your actions must be calculated to aid the mobilization of the workers and their allies and obstruct the mobilization of the fascists. The fascists are trying to do the same thing. They are trying to develop a system of tactics that will facilitate the mobilization of fascist forces and block the mobilization of our forces. Look at the line they are taking at San Francisco State. They are able to gull a lot of people who are raw material for the antifascist forces because of this mistake by the ultralefts.

This is no game for fools. This game is for all the marbles. The question is: is there going to be a victorious proletarian revolution or is there going to be fascism in power? The conscious forces on both sides know the game is for keeps.

It is important to keep these things in mind in

our discussions, to inculcate these lessons into our cadres and through our cadres into the mass movement. There's nothing wrong with the instincts of most of these young ultralefts. The instinct is in line with the task, that is, the destruction of the fascist forces. The problem is that they just do not know what time it is.

They remind me of grade school kids. An immeasurable number of black eyes and lost teeth are caused by the fact that youngsters don't know how to fight intelligently. They run in swinging their arms like a windmill. That's what these people are doing. But much more is at stake in this fight than there is in a schoolyard brawl.

We'll try to educate as many of them as we can but that's not the main thing. The main thing is to educate a growing army of antifascists. The issue at stake for every fighter is: Are you going to be ready for the real thing when it comes? And it will come.

Appendix

1. TWO LETTERS ON THE YOUTH COMMITTEE AGAINST FASCISM

Following is a 1934 exchange of letters between the Spartacus Youth League (SYL), the youth affiliate of the Communist League of America (CLA), and the Young People's Socialist League (YPSL), the youth group of the Socialist Party. The CLA was the first Trotskyist organization in the United States and a predecessor of the Socialist Workers Party. The letters were reprinted in the October 12, 1934, issue of the SYL's newspaper, *Young Spartacus*.

Fascist groups had begun to spring up in the United States in response to the economic crisis and the victory of Hitler in Germany. In opposing these initial fascist formations, the Trotskyists followed a policy aimed at building mass working-class countermobilizations against the fascists. To accomplish this, they realized, a united front of workers' organizations would be needed. The CLA and the SYL thus sought to apply the key lesson of the German workers' defeat.

The Stalinists and the Social Democrats opposed such a united front, as they had done in Germany. The Stalinists, still in their ultraleft "Third Period," held that all other working class organizations represented varieties of fascism.

The Social Democrats favored a class collaborationist approach to the fight against fascism, relying on alliances with liberals to preserve capitalist "democracy." Under intense pressure, the YPSL had engaged in a united-front antifascist action with the SYL on May 30, 1934. To evade the necessity of such activities, the YPSL leaders initiated the Youth Committee Against Fascism (YCAF). The main task of this organization was the issuance of social-democratic propaganda against fascism. The YPSL held that this was an adequate substitute for a united front of workers' organizations.

Thus the criticisms by the SYL of the YPSL and YCAF were well taken on all the key strategic questions in dispute. On the issue of democratic rights, however, the young Trotskyists made an error that parallels the error made by the Young Socialist Alliance at the beginning of a later period of class polarization. The letter to YPSL describes the objective of antifascist counterdemonstrations as preventing the fascists from "assembling and spreading their insidious program."

Similar formulations appeared in the SYL resolution, "Youth in the Struggle Against American Fascism," published in the December 1934 issue of *Young Spartacus*. The line of action proposed by the resolution was wholly correct: ". . . Our league should take the initiative to bring together the various youth organizations under a minimum program of action against Fascism, for the organization of united protest actions, mass meetings and counterdemonstrations, for the defense of the democratic rights of workers' organizations." The resolution concluded, however, by declaring that the "rights" of the fascists must be "taken away" by the workers.

The objective of the working class struggle against fascism is not to suppress the fascists' legal right to "spread" an insidious program, but to stop them from *carrying it out*. The fascists challenge the right of the *workers' organizations* to assemble and spread their program. The rights of the fascists are not at issue because it is not their rights that are under attack, but those of the working class. Erroneous formulations such as those used by the SYL in these instances could provide liberals and reformists with an excuse to falsely portray the workers' fight against fascism as an assault on democratic rights.

Experience has taught this lesson to the Trotskyist movement in the United States. In the more serious struggles against fascism that took place in 1938 and 1939, the Trotskyists of the Socialist Workers Party avoided slogans that could make it appear that the antifascists were trying to suppress anyone's rights. Instead, they realistically and honestly portrayed the battle against fascist goon squads as the defense of the hard-won democratic rights of the workers and their allies.

FROM **YOUNG SPARTACUS**

The Youth Committee Against Fascism has already had several months of sterile existence. Its failure is graphically displayed by the fact that it is not active in the anti-Fascist front in any section of the country. More than that, it is not even participating in such anti-Fascist actions as the Columbus Day demonstration on Oct. 12 in New York. Where is the need of an anti-Fascist organization which refrains from the anti-fascist activity?

The impotence of the Y.C.A.F. is due in most part and fundamentally to its false basis. The letter of the Spartacus Youth League clearly explains the position of our organization towards mass (individual membership) anti-Fascist organizations.

We believe that the struggle against Fascism requires a united front of working class organizations. The May 30th anti-war, anti-Fascist demonstration sponsored by the Y.P.S.L. and the Spartacus Youth League was a beginning towards the development of a national united front of youth. The Columbus Day united front of youth organizations is a continuation of this movement. We strive to convert these local united fronts into a national action of all working class youth organizations.

—*Editor*

Winston Dancis, Sec.
Young Peoples Socialist League
[address omitted]

Dear Comrade Dancis,

Our agreement to promote united front anti-war, anti-Fascist demonstrations on May 30th met with some success in several cities, particularly New York. Our Committee is prepared to participate in further efforts to construct a united front of youth organizations against war and Fascism which would include all sections of the radical, labor and student movement.

Along these lines we were ready to proceed in New York. Comrade Ben Fisher informed us that the Y.P.S.L. was not interested at the present time in continuing the "United Youth Committee Against War and Fascism" and considered the "Youth Committee Against Fascism" as sufficient to carry on the immediate anti-Fascist work.

We are therefore prompted to write to you on the "Y.C.A.F.". The questions and views presented are based on information and material supplied by comrade Fisher.

1. It is not clear as to precisely what organizations participated in the formation of the Y.C.A.F. On what basis were they selected and is the "National Council" open to further affiliations? If you intend getting further organization affiliations, what are the requirements, obligations and rights of these organizations?

2. We note that you aim to recruit individual adherents for the Y.C.A.F. who would spread its message "in school, shop, mill, mine, office and breadline". Are these supporters to be formed into groups which are federated on a regional and national scale? Are they to have the right, at a future date, to elect their own regional officers and committees as well as through a national conference elect the "National Council"? Comrade Fisher informed us that no conferences are being planned and the regional committees are being appointed by the National Council. Is this a temporary measure or is it intended as a permanent feature of the Y.C.A.F.?

For our part we do not see the value of a mass individual membership organization against Fascism. An individual membership organization can be based on a revolutionary program, or a liberal pacifist-program. We see no need to build a new membership organization against Fascism on a revolutionary program—we believe that that is the task of our Spartacus Youth League. As to a liberal pacifist anti-Fascist organization, it is obvious that such a formation would serve as an obstacle rather than an aid to genuine anti-Fascist work.

3. In our opinion this view is supported by the present program of the Y.C.A.F. It aims "to educate youth to understand the real nature of Fascism, and to work to end the conditions which have brought this reaction in Europe and also threaten us in America." Who can accomplish this task but a political revolutionary labor organization? Surely not a group on whose advisory committee are such liberals and pacifists as Franz Boas, Jerome Davis, John Dewey and Oswald Garrison Villard!

While a united front for definite anti-Fascist action is possible with these elements, if they represent organizations, a fundamental program which includes a basic analysis of Fascism and a clear cut position of how to avoid and combat it, is impossible unless we are to give up the essence of our own program.

The dangers of an organization such as the Y.C.A.F. is clearly shown in its program of "pledge". The individual adherent is asked to pledge—among other things—"to oppose attacks on civil, religious or radical liberties and to support equality and justice for all."

This pledge cannot be taken by any genuine anti-Fascist fighter. Is he going to defend the "civil liberties" of the Fascists? Is he to support "equality and justice" for the Fascists and the anti-Fascists? Arthur Garfield Hays, a liberal anti-Fascist, recently defended the civil rights of the Fascists to assemble in New Jersey. According to the program of the Y.C.A.F. this action should be supported. Then what becomes of counterdemonstrations to Fascist rallies?

In our opinion, it is important that, today when Fascism in the United States is still in its infancy as a movement, a mass movement of all anti-Fascist organizations and elements be organized to prevent, by all possible means, the growth of the murderous Fascist bands. This has meant and will mean physical clashes with the Fascists to prevent them from assembling and spreading their insidious program of the destruction of labor organizations and the denial of civil liberties for all anti-Fascists.

All attempts of Fascist bands to break working class meetings must be met with united front workers defense corps. But this is hardly sufficient. Immediate action to obstruct their "civil rights" to assemble forces which can effectively conduct such destructive activity is also needed. No true anti-Fascist can reject or overlook such a task.

The same liberal and constitutional sentence of the pledge is further objectionable to those like ourselves, and sections of your organization, who hold that a classless society is possible only through the medium of a transition period where the civil liberties, equality and justice of the present exploiting class, will be limited or entirely abrogated, that is, a dictatorship of the working class. In our opinion it is false to pose the demand for democratic rights today in such a liberal fashion.

We await an early reply to our questions and objections.

Fraternally
(Signed) Joseph Carter
Secretary

Letter of YPSL to YSL

August 3, 1934

Joe Carter
Spartacus Youth League
[Address Omitted]

Dear Comrade Carter.
The National Executive Committee of the Y.P.S.L. considered the letter which you sent on June 30 in regard to our anti-Fascist work and Youth Committee Against Fascism.

The Y.P.S.L. took a leading part in establishing the Y.C.A.F. in order to have a special organization that would carry on Anti-Fascist work.

We do not seek the affiliation of the Spartacus Youth League in this endeavor and will be active with other affiliated organizations in the Y.C.A.F. in order to carry on this line in regard with our objectives.

I believe that Bob Parker of New York will be able to give you any further information which you may wish.

Fraternally yours,
(Signed) Winston Dancis
National Secretary

2. WHY I AGREED TO APPEAR BEFORE THE DIES COMMITTEE (EXCERPT)

By Leon Trotsky

©1973 by Pathfinder Press, Inc. Reprinted by Permission.

The following article, written on March 11, 1939, first appeared in the December 30, 1939, issue of *Socialist Appeal*. It is reprinted from *Writings of Leon Trotsky [1939–40]* (New York: Pathfinder, 1973). The Dies Committee was the House Un-American Activities Committee headed by Texas Democrat Martin Dies.

Why did I agree to appear before the Dies Committee? Naturally not in order to facilitate the realization of Mr. Dies's political aims, particularly the passing of federal laws against one or another extremist "party." Being an irreconcilable opponent not only of fascism but also of the present-day Comintern, I am at the same time decidedly against the suppression of either of them.

The outlawing of fascist groups would inevitably have a fictitious character: as reactionary organizations they can easily change color and adapt themselves to any kind of organizational form since the influential sections of the ruling class and of the governmental apparatus sympathize considerably with them and these sympathies inevitably increase during times of political crisis.

As for the Comintern, suppression could only help this completely degenerated and compromised organization. The difficulty in the Comintern's situation is a result of the irreconcilable contradiction between the international workers' movement and the interests of the Kremlin ruling clique. After all its zigzags and deceptions, the Comintern has obviously entered its period of decomposition. The suppression of the Communist Party would immediately re-establish its reputation in the eyes of the workers as a persecuted fighter against the ruling classes.

However, the question is not exhausted by this consideration. Under the conditions of the bourgeois regime, all suppression of political rights and freedom, no matter whom they are directed against in the beginning, in the end inevitably bear down upon the working class, particularly its most advanced elements. That is a law of history. The workers must learn how to distinguish between their friends and their enemies according to their own judgment and not according to the hints of the police.

It is not difficult to predict an ad hominem objection: "But just that Soviet government in which you yourself took part proscribed all political parties except the Bolsheviks?" Entirely correct; and to this day I am ready to bear responsibility for its actions. But one cannot identify the laws of civil war with the laws of peaceful periods; the laws of the dictatorship of the proletariat with the laws of bourgeois democracy.

If one considered Abraham Lincoln's policy exclusively from the point of view of civil liberties, then the great president would not appear very favorably. In justification of course he could say that he was compelled to apply civil war measures in order to cleanse the democracy of slavery. Civil war is a state of tense social crisis. One or another dictatorship, inevitably growing out of the conditions of civil war, appears fundamentally as an exception to the rule, a temporary regime.

It is true that the dictatorship in the Soviet Union did not die out, but on the contrary took on monstrous totalitarian forms. This is explained by the fact that out of the revolution arose a new privileged caste which is incapable of maintaining its regime except through measures of a hidden civil war. It was precisely over this question that I broke with the Kremlin ruling clique. I was defeated because the working class, as a result of internal and external conditions, showed itself to be too weak to liquidate its own bureaucracy. I have, however, no doubt that the working class will liquidate it.

But whatever the situation in the USSR may be, the working class in the capitalist countries, threatened with their own enslavement, must stand in defense of freedom for all political tendencies including their own irreconcilable enemies. That is why I do not feel the slightest sympathy for the aims of the Dies Committee.

3. COMRADE CROSS INVENTS A PROBLEM (EXCERPT)
A Reply to "The Relationship Between Free Speech and the Proletarian Revolution"

By Felix Morrow

The following item is reprinted from SWP *Internal Bulletin* No. 8, May 1939. Felix Morrow was a member of the SWP Political Committee who wrote many of the key articles on fascism published in the *Socialist Appeal*, the SWP's twice-weekly newspaper, in 1939.

On February 20, 1939, the SWP led a demonstration of 50,000 protesting a fascist meeting at Madison Square Garden. Other political forces had abstained from the action, for fear of undermining their ties with New York's Mayor La Guardia.

Many liberals and Stalinist sympathizers tried to justify their refusal to participate in the antifascist demonstration by pretending that such demonstrations violated the fascists' right to free speech. This attempt to divert attention from the real issues was answered in "Should Fascists be Allowed the Right of Free Speech?", an unsigned article probably authored by Morrow, in the March 3, 1939, issue of the *Socialist Appeal*. Morrow also flayed the liberals for their failure to defend the civil rights of the antifascist demonstrators against brutal police attacks.

Stalinists claimed that the purpose of the antifascist demonstration was to prevent or break up the fascist meeting. Morrow answered this in the March 10, 1939, *Socialist Appeal:* "Jerome's reference to 'forcibly' preventing the meeting is of course a dishonest subterfuge; the issue involved was that of a counterdemonstration, of mass picketing of the meeting."

Roger Cross, a member of the SWP, interpreted the position taken by the SWP as *opposing* the application of free speech rights to fascists. In "Comrade Cross Invents a Problem," Morrow attempted to eliminate this misunderstanding.

☙

I have carefully read and reread Comrade Cross' article, "The Relationship Between Free Speech and the Proletarian Revolution" [see the same number of the *Bulletin*]. I regret that it is not a fruitful contribution to analyzing the new problems concretely raised by the slogan of Workers Defense Guards. That slogan does raise important new problems. Comrade Cross has, however, simply invented a nonexistent problem; he has done so, as I shall show, in order to propagate an historical interpretation of the Thermidorean reaction in Soviet Russia which is alien to the Trotskyist explanation of the degeneration of the workers state in Russia. The free speech "problem" invented by him serves merely as a springboard for a false historical theory. Comrade Cross is within his rights in raising any and all questions during the preconvention discussion. But the main body of his article is an argument against a straw man, for it is *not* true that the party "denies free speech to fascists"; while the real logical motivation of his article—the enunciation of an anti-Trotskyist explanation of the degeneration of the proletarian dictatorship in Russia—is simply asserted without a word of argument or proof.

Comrade Cross writes: "The current articles in the press of the SWP have unambiguously pledged that party to most violent action in smashing the fascists and in denying them the right to speak. A more thoughtful leadership would simply agitate to smash the fascists, and leave the question of their right to speak alone. The arguments used are: that the avowed object of the fascists is to smash all democratic rights. They would deny us the right to speak, put us in concentration camps and shoot us. Consequently, why should they be allowed free speech?"

Where did Comrade Cross find the *Socialist Appeal* saying that fascists should not be allowed to speak? He cites no issues and pages of the *Appeal*—and with good reason, for he could find no such citations. Yet he blandly reports the *Appeal*'s arguments for this nonexistent position.

A very fruitful discussion can be had on the extremely delicate problems connected with calling upon the workers to fight against the fascists: when to speak purely in defensive terms, and when to go over to terms indicating an offensive against the fascists. For the moment, it is clear, political realities—the speedy growth of the fascists, our own weakness—dictate defensive terms. A warning must also be given to the party against a too-technical conception of the formation of Workers Defense Guards: unless the Guards are merely the first ranks, carrying with them nonparty and nonguard elements in their actions, we shall find ourselves defeating the real purpose for mobilizing the guards: getting the masses to move with us. We must also convince the party membership—and above all the youth—that the guard is a practical, feasible, and pressing task. These and other problems deserve discussion. But not this invention of Comrade Cross.

It has long been clearly thought out, in the Bolshevik movement, where we stand on the question of free speech. First of all, "free speech" belongs to the category of "civil liberties." Let those who will, engage in this activity—we certainly don't denounce the *existence* of the American Civil Liberties Union—but the task of the revolutionist and of the working class and its allies is the fight for the *democratic rights of the working class.*

From the concept of "civil liberties," the American Civil Liberties Union logically arrives at the point of offering its services to fascists who in isolated instances run afoul of a progressive mayor or police chief. What do we say about such actions of the ACLU? We say: for every fascist persecuted by the state, ten thousand workers are persecuted. We are ready to tell the ACLU of more cases of workers' rights being violated than the ACLU can possibly handle. The ACLU knows this as well as we. But the ACLU is so anxious to prove its respectability, so fawningly worried about the good opinion of bosses and their stooges, that the ACLU takes good money and lawyers that might be used to help persecuted workers, and diverts it to the use of the fascists.

This concrete criticism of the ACLU does not involve a denial of free speech to the fascists. Moreover, is it our business to tell the capitalist state what to do about the fascists, to please give them free speech? Not at all. We give advice only to the workers, and we call upon them to fight fascism. The only point at which we will suppress the free speech of the fascists is only in the broad sense that, in carrying out the seizure of state power, we shall undoubtedly have to smash the fascist organizations and suppress the fascist cadres.

4. POLITICAL REPORT TO THE JUNE 1961 SWP CONVENTION (EXCERPT)

By Farrell Dobbs

Reprinted from *SWP Discussion Bulletin*, Vol. 22, No. 19, September 1961

The current outbreak of rightist movements—Youth for Goldwater, John Birch Society, the extremist American Nazis, etc.—requires close attention and it also poses some tactical questions that need clarification. Implicit in this trend is the ultimate danger of repressive fascist attacks on labor and its allies, against which the labor movement will have to wage a showdown struggle in the streets. But it would be a serious mistake to raise a hue and cry against incipient fascism, as though the ultimate danger were already upon us, and attempt to substitute ourselves for the masses in taking the issue to the streets here and now. National politics still remains class collaborationist in mass character, despite the growing restiveness of labor and its allies. While this class political equilibrium remains operative, fascism can't make significant headway. When the present equilibrium does become upset through a labor breakaway from capitalist politics, it does not necessarily follow that capitalism will resort forthwith to fascist measures. An attempt might be made, as class political antagonism sharpen, to establish bonapartist rule, perhaps through a military dictatorship based on the present vast interlocking alliance between the officer corps and the monopoly capitalists. Fascist trends would receive strong new impulses at such a conjuncture, but the ultimate showdown with fascism would still not be at hand. Therefore our propaganda, in addition to explaining the meaning of fascism and educating the masses in the need to be on guard against it, must also analyze the complex interim questions of the power struggles which could be next on the agenda.

At the present time, given the class collaborationist character of national politics, the existing rightist formations simply represent vanguard polarizations on the right which play the counterpart of our vanguard role on the left. They can do little more than conduct propaganda, resorting only to isolated, small scale acts of hooliganism which often backfire against them. Since the incipient fascists are not strong enough to carry through antidemocratic actions at present, a call for mobilization against them would give the general impression of an attempt on our part to suppress freedom of speech and assembly for others. We would not only be inviting comparable attacks, both legal and extra-legal, against our own democratic rights, but we would appear to have given them justification. The truth is that we stand for freedom of speech and assembly in principle—not just for us, but for everybody. Therefore, we do not demand that the rightist movements be denied these freedoms.

Concerning the question of civil liberties, we should keep in mind that our growing reputation as a serious revolutionary tendency with a meaningful program is drawing attention not only from people becoming radicalized. The witch hunters are taking notice as well. We are beginning to draw their fire to a new degree in connection with the Cuban defense movement and there could be other new attacks. More than ever we must be on guard against any undermining of civil liberties for all, if we hope to defend our own democratic rights. To act otherwise would be to repeat the costly mistake of the Stalinists in refusing to recognize the democratic rights of their political opponents.

Let me call to your attention an article Trotsky wrote on this subject in December 1939 in the *Socialist Appeal* under the title, "Why I Consented to Appear Before The Dies Committee." I don't have the time to give you the background but it's worth your while to go back and do a little research on the circumstances surrounding the question of Trotsky possibly testifying before the

Dies Committee, intending to use the occasion for propaganda purposes.

The questions of Stalinist dictatorship, of democratic rights under capitalism and the policy of revolutionists on civil liberties in a capitalist country like ours came up in this discussion. Trotsky wrote in the article cited, "Being an irreconcilable opponent not only of fascism but also of the present-day Comintern, I am at the same time decidedly against the suppression of either of them." He pointed out that the suppression of fascists by the capitalist government always proves fictitious. He also took note of the fact that to defend the rights of the Stalinists could help to refurbish the Comintern. "However," he said, "the question is not exhausted by this consideration. Under the conditions of the bourgeois regime, all suppression of political rights and freedom, no matter whom they are directed against in the beginning, in the end inevitably bear down upon the working class, particularly its most advanced elements. That is a law of history."

In the article Trotsky was speaking of a specific stage, the one we're in now, where we're struggling under adverse conditions against a repressive ruling class in a capitalist country. He pointed out that when the struggle intensifies into a class showdown a new factor arises, the rules of civil war, which are something else again. But concerning a situation such as ours, he stated unambiguously ". . . the working class in the capitalist countries, threatened with their own enslavement must stand in defense of freedom for all political tendencies including their own irreconcilable enemies."

Under circumstances where the foregoing policy will be maintained, we may at times find it useful propagandistically to organize counter-demonstrations against incipient fascists. In any situation where they resort to rightist hooliganism we will take the initiative in organizing defense guards to oppose them. But our central task at this stage concerning the rightist formations is to explain the true nature of fascism in our propaganda, seeking to educate and alert the masses against it. In doing so we must keep a sense of proportion as to the immediate nature of the fascist issue, being careful to direct major attention to the primary questions of the day.

EXPAND YOUR REVOLUTIONARY LIBRARY

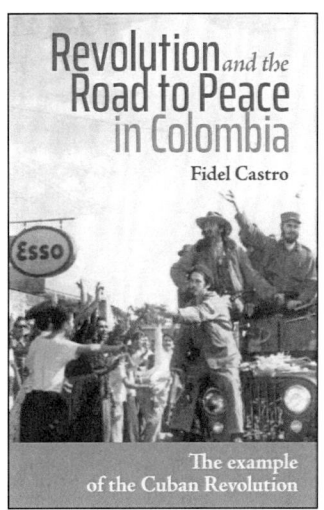

New!
Revolution and the Road to Peace in Colombia
The Example of the Cuban Revolution
FIDEL CASTRO

"No crime can be committed in the name of revolution," Fidel Castro declares, drawing from the example set by working people of Cuba as they took state power out of the hands of its capitalist rulers. In 2008, as part of efforts to end six decades of armed conflict in Colombia, he shared the exemplary record of Cuba's revolutionary struggle with the Revolutionary Armed Forces of Colombia (FARC) and the world. $10. Also in Spanish.

New Expanded Edition!
Cosmetics, Fashion, and the Exploitation of Women
MARY-ALICE WATERS
JOSEPH HANSEN, EVELYN REED

"Norms of beauty and fashion are inseparable from the class struggle." That's the title of the opening chapter of this timely new edition of a lively 1950s debate in the Militant, a socialist newsweekly. How cosmetics and fashion monopolies rake in profits from social insecurities of women and adolescents. Why women's integration into the workforce and unions is a major advance in the fight for emancipation. A Marxist classic on the origins of women's oppression and the working-class road forward. $15. Also in Spanish, French, Farsi, Greek.

Fascism: What It Is and How to Fight It
LEON TROTSKY

Writing in the heat of struggle against the rising fascist movement in Europe in the 1930s, Russian communist leader Leon Trotsky examines the origins and nature of fascism and advances, for the first time, a working-class strategy to combat and defeat it. $5. Also in Farsi.

Imperialism's March Toward Fascism and War
JACK BARNES

"There will be new Hitlers, new Mussolinis. That is inevitable. What is not inevitable is that they will triumph. The working-class vanguard will organize our class to fight back against the devastating toll we are made to pay for the capitalist crisis. The future of humanity will be decided in the contest between these contending class forces." In *New International* no. 10. $14. Also in Spanish, French, Farsi, Greek.

The Teamster Series
FARRELL DOBBS

Four books on the 1930s strikes, organizing drives, and political campaigns that transformed the Teamsters into a militant industrial union movement. Written by the organizer of these battles and leader of the Socialist Workers Party. A tool for workers seeking to use union power and advance the fight for a party of labor. $16 each, series $50. Also in Spanish. *Teamster Rebellion* is also available in French, Farsi, Greek.

50 Years of Covert Operations in the US
Washington's Political Police and the American Working Class
LARRY SEIGLE, FARRELL DOBBS
STEVE CLARK

How class-conscious workers have defended constitutional freedoms and fought the capitalists' drive to build the "national security" state essential to maintaining their rule. $10. Also in Spanish and Farsi.

PATHFINDERPRESS.COM

Opening Guns of World War III: Washington's Assault on Iraq
JACK BARNES

The murderous assault on Iraq in 1990–91 heralded increasingly sharp conflicts among imperialist powers, growing instability of capitalism, and more wars. Also includes:

1945: When US Troops Said 'No!' by Mary-Alice Waters

Lessons from the Iran-Iraq War by Samad Sharif

In *New International* no. 7. $14. Also in Spanish, French, Farsi.

Lenin's Final Fight
Speeches and Writings, 1922–23
V.I. LENIN

In 1922 and 1923, V.I. Lenin, central leader of the world's first socialist revolution, waged what was to be his last political battle—one that was lost after his death. At stake was whether that revolutionary government and the world communist movement it led would remain on the revolutionary proletarian course that brought workers and peasants to power in Russia in 1917. $17. Also in Spanish, Farsi, Greek.

The Fight Against Fascism in the USA
Forty Years of Struggle Described by Participants
JAMES P. CANNON

In 1939 some 50,000 people in New York City responded to a call by the Socialist Workers Party to answer a pro-Nazi rally of 20,000. "The question of how to fight fascism was answered in thunderous tones by the magnificent demonstration which raised the cry: Workers Defense Guards to crush the fascist danger!" $5

The Socialist Workers Party in World War II, 1940–43
JAMES P. CANNON

Preparing the communist workers movement in the United States to campaign against wartime censorship, repression, and anti-union assaults. $23

The Spanish Revolution (1931–39)
LEON TROTSKY

Trotsky recounts a decade of revolutionary struggles and the Stalinist betrayal in Spain that ensured a fascist victory in 1939, making World War II inevitable. $23

Cuba and the Coming American Revolution
JACK BARNES

This is a book about the example set by the Cuban people that socialist revolution is not only necessary—it can be made. A book about the struggles of workers and other exploited producers in the imperialist heartland, and the youth attracted to them. About the class struggle in the US, where the revolutionary capacities of working people are as utterly discounted by the ruling powers as were those of the Cuban toilers. $10. Also in Spanish, French, Farsi.

Pathfinder Press **accessible e-books** for the blind, those with low vision, or other challenges reading print books

For a list of current accessible titles, go to: pathfinderpress.com/collections/books-for-the-blind.

Visit bookshare.org for information on how to sign up.